Data Trace

RONNIE MCGRATH is a Creative Writing Lecturer at Imperial College London and the University of The Arts, London College of Communication. A former musician, he was a founding member of the defunct musical group the *London Afro Blok*, who toured Europe, performed for the Queen and opened the 1994 Commonwealth Games in British Columbia, Canada. In 1993, he was commended for his writing by *ACER*, who later published and awarded first place for his writing in 1994. As a contemporary artist, he has exhibited his work throughout London.

Also by Ronnie McGrath:

CD Acoustic Avant-Gardism: streams of consciousness poems for neo-surrealists (ankhademia press, 2008)
On the Verge of Losing iT (ankhademia press, 2005)
Poems For the Tired Lips of Newspapers, (The Tall-lighthouse Press 2003, 2005, 2007)
The Day Before That One, Too, in IC3 *The Penguin Book of New Black Writing in Britain,* (Penguin 2000)

Data Trace

by

RONNIE MCGRATH

S
SALT
CAMBRIDGE

PUBLISHED BY SALT PUBLISHING
14a High Street, Fulbourn, Cambridge CB21 5DH United Kingdom

Salt Publishing 2010

Printed in Great Britain by the MPG Books Group, Bodmin and King's Lynn

Typeset in Swift 9.5 / 13

ISBN 978 1 84471 469 8 paperback

1 3 5 7 9 8 6 4 2

for
Daisy, Lulu, Mali & Kimeya

Contents

Acknowledgements

Among other things, insight and inspiration has come from my mother Joyce—her love, home cooking and spirituality; from my wife, Daisy – her love, love, love and continuous love and support; from my children—worship the air they breathe; from my brother Donovan and his wife Lauren—their love, support, conversation and advice on healthy eating; from Anthony Joseph—his complexity and for turning me onto some great poetry; from my fellow poets—their jealousy and envy, only joking guys. *Beautiful people all of you!* A special thanks to everyone at Salt.

'The worst crime is faking it.'
—KURT COBAIN

'You must surrender whatever preconceptions you have about music if you're really interested in it.'
—CECIL TAYLOR

'To live means to leave traces.'
—WALTER BENJAMIN

'. . . what was silent will speak, what is closed will open and will take on a voice.'
—PAUL VIRILIO

On Becoming A Poet

in dream I listened
    to an impossible music
        with an impossible melody
            it curled around my tongue
                (me thinking of a phoenix)
                    put the fire in my mouth
                      feel the peace?
                          creation is cure.

Diasfrican

I put myself on the line and might never be published/might
never be liked/might never be needed/my poetry wild as
innovation/lights ablaze with language/reservoirs of some
radical speech act/ emotions running high/rich in haiku-
globin/in and out of form/jouissance/buck wild and naked
poetry art/untamed voice of some past etching seeping through
my verse/alphabetically coded fridge magnets waking me from
sleep/ from psychotherapy/from costume dramas of Freudian
dream tablets/scopophilic movie houses/spray painting rooms
with manifestos of dada-glyphics /manifestos of hierarchical-
glyphics/the spectacle of spectacle poems looking back on
Sankofa birds/the past of our present findings/trapped
here/in a culture of wires and technology/tuning me
in/dropping me out/tuning me in/dropping me out/my
eyes of computer screens/a virtual surface noise in saliva and
steel/tattooed body armour/expressionist fish scale/broken
off/ severed / amputated / i am   closed / hermetically
sealed/persona non-grata/fucked/putting myself on the
line/a textile pattern in fluorescent daybreak/writing in
some Jackson Pollock rendition of serendipity/scratched
upon flesh of palimpsest scars/superimposed ancient
graffiti paintwork/older than cobwebs/than lime scale/than
numerals/than times infinity/than repetition/the tattooed
language of needle tongues/the knife-sharp language of
expletives/like the speed driven bodies of crashed cars/swollen
vehicles/beaten into submission/beaten into pan/beaten
into calypso and rhythm/sparrows news item mightier than
a sword/a weh di man wid de hammer go?/tell me/a weh
di man wi di hammer go?/Nubian cyborgs of my peoples
language in plumes of exotic affluenza/ contagious offerings
to the high priestess/to the vernacular women of vernacular

cultures/interneti-zens of the virtual world/carnivores of some female paradissimo/putting me on the line/my locality global/got me thinking in the general and the specific of these paradigm shifts/my linguistic furnishing/my linguistic clothes/the hypertextualised transsexual frameworks of some rapid ear movement/eavesdropping on rippled water/exoteric silk circles in the guise of magic/vignetted shades of the plain and silent shapes of things to come/

The Catalyst: Ode to Sun Ra

Your burst of Sun Ra is an incredible drinking water of ebony
rain capsules imprinted on the sun-baked earth in a golden
footfall of glorious experimentation / the future of your
visions are with us now / colouring the air with renditions of
the peacocks tail feathers / the ankh-like features of my black
nose hip to your frankincense and hip to your myrrh / the
incense smoke of your spirituality / enveloping my soul with
the ineffable fingerprints of jazz compositions / communicating
in polysemic voices of genre music / polysemic voices of
rage / polysemic voices of peace makers / throwing splashes of
minkisi medicine into the minds of abstract oil painters / the
coded universe of your signs and your symbols is an intense
language of no compromise / I know you would rather die
alone than drown a slow death in this watered down version
of reality / the straight world of conformity was never for
you / you were not seduced by the superfluous skins of their
fashion houses / and unlike the so-called revolutionaries of this
artistry / you did not even succumb to the scent of their bank
notes / that green obsession of man-made isms / capitalisms
food mountains stacked like burger piles of cash / hamburgers
of obesities screening off like the Hollywood effect of a hit
movie in this primitive world of logo-centrism / ritualistic
earth practice of bizarre hierarchies / mannequins of
oppression / taxonomising children with the jewels of their
clothes / sexualised garments of intricate lace patterns / black
lace colourings cooler than negritude / black lace colourings
of exoticism / black lace colourings of mobile telephone
masts / pirating the airwaves / subverting culture with a push
towards the new frontiers of futuristic travellers on their
way to Sun Ra country / the DNA of avant-guardism / where
theory meets practice and practice makes perfection out of

your finest art/ark-works of Noah's crossing into the sublime
landscapes of a new music hidden in an eyeball/the stuff
of light bulbs emanating from the keys with smooth sound
textures tasting like skin blisters when set down upon the
stones of tongues/tongue textures feeling like a woman in
slow motion/feeling like a woman in song/her voice/bouncing
off the wall/exploding in my ear like the secret language of a
whisper/I offer her a butterfly and still she smears my lips with
the herstories of a womanist fiction/heterodiegetic narratives of
the pharaohs coming/premonitions of black star liners shaping
out of the sky like the indelible mark of a comet/shaping
out of the sky like an ankh/pyramids of geometric sand
dunes sticking out of the desert in the breast-like features of
thorns/she beckons me to mine this African flesh of a rich
mineral earth/subcutaneous rivers of invention forcing eczema
to appear on the outer frames of mountain bikes/the intensity
of your music is just one of the roads which I have walked to
meet her here/she a treasure trove of stanza patterns/she the
automatic writing of my soul inscribed upon a wish to be free
in life and in art/she much more than just some empty play
of words/she an ode to you Sun Ra/myth maker and master of
invention/the catalyst/he who changes everything but forever
stays the same/

Black Orchid Milk

(ode to Anthony Joseph)

brother from another planet
       your roving camera eye fixed on future habits
       roots and routes
         the inevitable rays of a wise sunlight
your rhythm simple in its complex encomium to abstraction

Satchmo's Lips

Unzip this rain cloud/watch the sun bleach out of it like the burning fires of illumination pushed into a trumpet solo/notated speech patterns hollering from the fields of southern trees/blowing in the southern breeze of profound sound sculptures fucking with the visceral undercurrents of my unconsciousness/the unconscious rivers of my psyche succumbs to your music/succumbs to your poetry/succumbs to your mind treatment/the psychiatry of your fingers dancing in the key of G/your witchdoctor music of toes and feathers/of frog spawn and frogs legs/of rabbit foot/of chicken blood/of horses hair/of bones and feathers smeared upon your lips like an Arkestra of invention in the blue black world of free expression and pentatonic handshakes/hanging from the pants of youth culture/MTV designer children sharp as torch-lights/cutting through the swamp land with their razor deep laser beams harvesting sugarcane in the merciless heat of sweat and toil/cutting through/so very near to the thing that turns to gold/and yet/so very divorced from the herstories of their mothers washboards/from the herstories of their fathers captivity/from the herstories of ZONG/men over board/we're in the black again/we're in this bell of a trumpet mouth pushed out like the fleshy lips of a coloured boys nostril/and when his tears have washed away these food mountains/a watermelon smile known as black face is the only sound of laughter breaking through the illusion/ Hollywood screen culture/everywhere at once scenting their brand names with the smell of avarice/everywhere at once scenting their brand names with the smell of some watered down version of hyper-reality/where the media babes/tough as calf muscles hit on sports cars/take them home and dismantle their engine parts/sexy car seats dressed in leather/love making/cyborg style/cyborg women with metal hips blowing kisses to electric pylons/naked cyborg women swimming in the irrational rivers of my unconscious fantasies/fantasies of digital display units plugged into a market force/outsourcerers working their magik with simulacrums of vodun temples/syncretic versions of Afroceatic wizardry simulacrumised in this media mind game of a matrix prison house/I'm out there/thinking in the rag-time music of gumbo canvas works/thinking in the Pollock narratives of Louis' smile/Dionysian timbres of angelic trumpet notes/splashes of golden brass music sounding off like the sepia ring tones of Satchmo's lips pinned against his mouthpiece/freedom in an air shaft/and all that Jazz/and all that Jazz of accumulative rage and accumulative chaos/ushering poems to the foreground of black invention.

Poem for Ani-Difranco

The perpetual rhythm of everything

Night after night

Day after day
Of an endless wash cycle

Clothes upon clothes of baptism
Drowning in faith

Too much religion in the world

Too many poets
Art for arts sake dross of solipsism

Genius mind of skilful fingers
Birth meaningful songs from your womb

From the cave of your guitar lung

Wooden sound chamber heaven
Smelling like a woman

The revolution is a girl
A twelve year old Peruvian sex worker

War is so bloody

And men are not just cruel to themselves.

Elocutionary Tongues in Obedience of Language

I awake from the dreamy landscape of image and
song/me a poet/eyes bright as the wild sunlight of its own
inventiveness/ecstatic breaths in hues of purple/shimmers of
ochre with hands like footprints/on the plastic road of a plastic
tarmac/where the cruel breeze is a storm in waiting/nature
is muscle bound/pumped up/ and out of her mind/the
beauty of her forest dense with metal/dense with stone/feral
creatures of a wild and impossible night/all seeing/all
knowing/infinite stars in degrees and circles/gestures of some
rare and impenetrable body armour/gestures of an outmoded
theatre language/speaking to me in a foreign cuisine/good
life menu food/property ladders climbing out of holes/deep
ether in tenors and opera songs/the dizzying heights of
cultures in contention/elocutionary tongues in obedience of
language/ethnicity bound/our laughter/my laughter/your
laughter/their laughter/an intense moment of intricate
successes/of intricate excesses /explosions in textures of
drunken happiness/fragile as bone/fragile as buildings/fragile
as an intense silence in the image of fantasm/crawling into her
thighs like the children's children of my future lovers/bound
by whips on ships to the new world of pain and paradise/the
commodified fingers of their cruel habits/serving veins to
the narcotic effect of their nihilisms/the death drive of their
uncompromising youth/ seeking refuge in the self mutilatory
groves of guns and bullet wounds/deep/dark/ugly poem
of my pen/sheeted images of your truth/ image upon image
piled like corpses/plumes of indefinite melancholy/dim as the
sick moon/thin as the sick night/weak straws in search of air
holes/drowning world in the belly of a coin/our future/spent

Perfect One

My tongue is the language of a contemporary code
It is the poetry of my status in this land that I call home
I am versed in the fist upon knuckles of Black genius hands
turning vinyl scratch marks into the ebony gods of a joyful noise

The post-postmodernisms of tomorrows future is a little
    closer now
As I cut the beat and rewind to the future of
A Black technology known as Phunk

Philosophunk
The drum and the bass of Black expressionism
The scarification of electromagnetisms lighting up the sound
    waves
In a plethora of genre music

Lighting up the billboards in an orgy of negative advertising
    striving
To shut the future down

Black Dogonic future of space travellers
Their wide Black eyes long as shadows
Staring into a better world than this

Ndebele world of village art
Ndebele world of pure geometry
Ndebele world of eye poetry and ear paintings
Sounding out like the Afro futurisms of Sun Ra's musik

His compound narratives shaped like the faint outlines
Of a ballet dancer high on culture

Her language
Esoteric
Powerful
Abstract
Weird
Like the swords of her privilege
To walk upon the toes of prolific fingers
Ebony fingers shaped like fists
Punching holes into wedding rings.

Extract From A Charlie Parker Solo

One day we will meet in a place where silence is lighter than a feather and peace is the perfected outer-flow of a perfect music wrapped inside the protective universe of a single drop of rain/clinging to my eyelash as the world of my pupil descends/like an orange fruit dreaming of sunsets painting moles onto the rooftops of the beautiful houses/all of them virginal in the finite architecture of their frames/trapped inside the man-made bone of geometry/taller than steel/than metal/than mud huts and mud dusty lining in some brick work structure of conventionality/I build a wall around my heart to keep this house in order/families and homes are what makes my street come to life when the darkness has gone and the sudden lights of electric sky clouds make ripples appear on the gills of Negro truck drivers/fluorescent road maps delivering the city to the corporate cool of barcode factories/superfluous fish stockings lining the shelves with the strict discipline of horizontalism/the sharp gaze of my reading glasses/peering light years into the future/penetrating rainforests with a thousand pine needles protruding from my hairline/cutting oxygen/depleted air supply/my death a raw experimentation/my death an improvisation/12345678910/breath returns with the texture of sand dunes ground into mirror skin/the smoked filled rooms of my sunglasses/aborted/devoid of house coats/devoid of religion/consumerism pushed deep into the eye-sockets like the blunt aftershock of cherry pickers/their toe-like fingers smelling of vagina caves/penis envy the purpose of their lips/sexy conversations pushed against the purity of a secret language coded in the wedding gowns of tradition/woman I see you now/not in a painting but with the scent of angels releasing fingerprints into the air/this is your time/and i/lesser than a book/am loving your complexity/I see in the monologue of you polyrhythmic tongue twisters more versatile than gym slippers/the bone deep of you is like a fire in my mouth/my mouth ablaze with praise for you/fire mouth with fire people on the backs of comets/heading your way baby/gonna bathe your feet in text messages/gonna climb your ribs/pick your lock/open your cage/who needs to be rational when there are enough holes in the air to climb towards your love/who needs to be rational when there are enough holes in the air to seduce these tongues of mine/who needs to be rational when we can throw rooftops onto the necks of undernourished tower blocks/who needs to be rational when the space between our clothes is a multitude of safe houses/I guess we are in it for the long haul/you/me/and the magic of this page/your body is a mind trap/a conduit to self expression/you are a work in progress/and I will pick for you umbrella stems/to keep you dry when the rain comes/

How Di Body?

constructed engine parts of me
soul entombed by meat and membrane
vessels into vein storm

radikal oxygen shafts ferrying life capsules in tablet forms of
                                                    medicine men
shamanic spirit don't need possession
material things lean heavy on bone
inflexible ivory with a broken cast

climb these ribs to praise my God on steep mountain top
meditation smelling of peace pipe and tranquillity
my people need a break / man
finger pop their joyful noise
teach mouth-organs how to smile
push the darkness aside

sunlight threaded through a button hole

if the flowers really are alive
we must all eat dirt

Milford's Paradiddle

You promised to dismantle the world with your poems/so that when I got here/I could sprinkle drum solos onto this red earth and watch the rhythm of your feet dance the pain out of slavery/but the bag lady did not know the worth of those pages/the ones she tore from your book to fill the space between her toes/raising your words to her lips/ she extracts the liquid of your language/her moistured mouth exoticised/ And now that she is as wise as the sun could ever be/scarab beetles go to her in the guise of an ancient candle light/the eternal flames of their music speaking in paraddidles/six-eight yoroba facial scars quaint as laughter lines/reaching for the high-hat in a textured moment of sugar cane plantation songs/turning surface noise into the punctuated air flow of an Albert Ayler solo/Albert and Trane riding the keys of their horns/the immaculate conception of a new music/music of faith/music of hope hung upon the cross of experimentation/the black holes of their genius minds rich in sour-sop juice/diaspora seeds tied with Kora strings and scattered like a drum solo/drum solo music dissecting rain drops/drum solo music pulling rain drops through your sweat glands/paradiddles hitting the ground like a storm/ paradiddles hitting the ground like a storm compressing mind space into a single grain of sand/the intensity of your living gives form to light /wisdom in a paradigm/ the pain of your free expression hidden in a note/I hear that song/I have listened over and over until it suddenly rained on me like ideas I had never thought of/master drummer man, you/griot/poet/colour me blue as the purple mouths of Negro compositions so I can sew umbilical chords onto the lids of spy satellites/teach me how to space travel and I will show you that a drum can talk/talking drums of the unconscious mind swallowing sound capsules/electronic sound waves into your head space/radio head space/mind metaling/mineral rich ensemble food ontologically rooted in the key of life/the endless sky of your virtuosity mutating out of the black silence in a black magic invention of praise poems bending spoons as jimi feeds back on me/light years into a future of Afro-headed sound creatures/nesting deep in the waxy well of my sentient eardrum.

Acoustic Avant-Gardism
Streams of consciousness poems for neo-surrealists

I wonder as I wander in the non-linear hours of the soul / bent again / over tombs and a famished earth / bent again under lamps of illumination / a fluorescent daybreak of new poetries / where the rain tastes like melancholy / and the metallic flesh of our metal dreams roll off the production line / into the certainty of even more uncertainties / dead autonomy of an imprisoned freedom / freedoomed again / by a dusty rain without clothes / without shores to cling to / the pain of interest rates / dismantling homes / brick by brick devolutionary acts of disempowerment / the politricks of Pinochio's nose flowing like rivers of blood speeches / nations crossing nations in the porous borders of skin folds / miscegenated body fluids offend / who / not me / how dark are your children / how white are the truths of their eyes / sick metal of my own reflection looking back at me from the prosperity of mineral water / from the privilege of clothes / taste distinction of some indomitable class struggle subjugating race theory / subjugating feminisms / patriarchal tongue twisters speaking in man talk / walking the man walk of a precious slipper / synopticans of admiration / oh the love of cars / show me a woman who smells of gasoline / of steel / and wheels / of speed / and fibre glass / and I will phallic her symbols with an industrial age / power her climax with the hiss of dollar signs / build temples of the golden calf on heat / and what of god the community in disguise / can you out-stare the sun / can you / my brother? / then remove your shades and smell this poem / fluorescent daybreak of dense forest fires pasted on my fingers / the ivory keys of some grand piano / acoustic avant-gardisms fluttering like a solo in the brass of hummingbirds / nursing hurricanes as my fathers nose bleeds across the sheets /

Blood

I slice this vein and pour meaning
into things innumerable
signifiers as naked as a woman's shoe
scrape yesterdays lipstick
from the bonnets of their fingernail

Black sky bluer than when the sun was born
gives birth to infinite planets
voracious appetites devour birdseeds
and as the treacle of blood trickles across the page
dying becomes the norm of things unspoken

I slice this vein and pour meaning
into things immeasurable
footprints more abstract than flower stems
set their homes on dusty bookshelves

Orange day sun guard
vulnerable wombs from themselves
as the youngest of black revolutionaries
pour the narrative of their struggles
into the corporate hands of a microphone

I slice this vein and pour meaning
into things unclear, mouth-organs
unfettered by the guise of illusory habits
grin metal teeth fantastically
morning sky sucks rice grain through a straw
as the rational ways of celebrity poets
break the spirited charge of wild horses.

Mingus Music Act I

Marvellous tears of drinking water/lips sweeter than
sunlight/thirst driven back to whence it came/rested now/in
these voluptuous notes of sculptured music tastes/the
cushion calm of warm voices softer than air/air with holes
punched into them/the trumpeted holes of black music
spinning webs of complexity onto the hermetic texts of
fabulation/metafictitious narratives in songs of libations to the
spirit world/how I dig your mingus music/heartfelt bass lines
of Black star liners on their way to electric lady land/Beboptetic
rhythms in paradigms of album titles/the some kind of blue
of a Miles Davis solo/the Dr Funkenstein of Bootsy Collins sun
glasses/mother ships of invention/connecting us to the Fela
Kutinous horns of an Afro Beating steel pans into song/call
and response patterns frying hair do's in the Saturday night
fish fry of pomade fountains/smelling of burnt ice cream
cones/come symphony of flutes in a cacophony of rainbows
flushing through an airshaft in an instantaneous charge of
miraculous wisdom/come ensemble drummers with the stick
and palm of your wolof traditions pressing leaves into the
handprints of Bata rhythms/come you stringed instruments
of braided fingers and braided hair sprinkling Kora seeds
into the rich gumbo mix of multiculturalism/come you
radical expressionists of free jazz/come you poets of high
modernism/come you writers and ventriloquists/let us bop
to this Mingus music like it were our swan song/dense art
work opaque in its insight/broken egg shells with the cracked
offerings of reality seeping out of it/electric plugs with teeth
missing/dead car batteries on acid/streams of unconsciousness
dreaming art works of non-linearity/when it rains it bleeds
tears/rivers of black tarmac roads on the edible hooks of
carnivorous fishing lines/make this catch a big band/Duke

Ellington big/loose tubes empty as skeleton bones/the witch doctors crystal ball/trumpet features blowing lip bubbles into saliva streams/surreal renditions of the lobsters tale/he who is a conduit to the complex web of silk makers/he who is a miracle music/he who is the religious undertones of a crafted art work/he who configures in the anticipation of serendipity/literary dream-works/literary dream-works/ literary dream-works in repetitions of culture/cultures of some higher living/memories of vertiginous tower blocks/blowing up like canon fire/Beautiful lips of a jazz singer with microphone in hand/lecterns of her church music/her body shaped like an instrument/double bass machines in the key of thighs/eyes like a digital display unit/automated timbres of ice packs peppered with wasp stings/making love to a vein with capitalism in my pocket/trick bags of escapism/heroin highs/poverty lows/a culture in contention/nodding this groove/nodding this beat/beat/beat/ skibideeedooowap jazz/yeah/the shoes of the fisherman's wife are some jive ass slippers*

* title of a composition taken from the Charles Mingus album, *Let My Children Hear Music*

Hi-koo

This/ text/ makes/ no/ sense
For lan/guage/ is/ hid/den in
A/false/im/pres/sion

Of/re/a/li/ty
Ex/is/ting/out/side/of/thought
Out/side/ of/ meaning

Gi/ven/ to/ us/ in
Sym/bols/ and/ punc/tu/ation
Scratch/ marks/ of/ process

In/ten/ded/ mean/ing
Un/der/stood/ by/ the/ many
Who/ can/ read/ the/bones

And/ know/ their/ world/ is
A/highly/me/di/a/ted
Cut/up/of/all/things

Vis/u/al/and/texts
Con/struc/ted/for/the/reel/2
Reel/of/ci/ne/ma

Mingus Music Act II

Bones and trumpet notes/water-melanin music climbing
out of holes/climbing out of pipes/beautiful airshaft of
winged spirits in the company of flutes/intricate fingers of
feminine slippers blown from glass/cymbals of fire infesting
the drummers stick with paradiddles of rain falling on the
rusty roofs of aborted shanty towns/the music begins with
polemics of black nationalisms/some call it a cliché/but we
all know that it is a free jazz composition purchased on credit
cards/revolution for sale/long live consumerism/power to
the beetle/PAUSE!/there is a silence here/there is a complicit
silence here/there is a deafening silence here/can you hear
it?/the music begins with brush strokes/textures of Pablo
Picasso/Diego Velázquez/Beauford Delaney/and Jean-Michel
Basquait/I was coloured once/pretty as a painting/but now
I speak in the postmodern tongues of urbanity/symbols
of youth culture in the non-static order of contemporary
language/black speech-flows colonising microphones
with gumbo talk/syncretic angel feathers lost in their own
dreams/rhythms of themselves simulacrumised /Bones and
trumpet notes/Negropolitanarianisms/strolling through
my thoughts in an iambic pentameter of unadulterated
Phunk/Philosophunk/a metafictitiously wonderful head
space of untreated fabulation/of fiction gone wild/poet
trees shedding their autumnal leaves as the provocative
landscapes of her female anatomy comes gliding through
the science fiction of long tunnels/there isn't even time to
count my eye-lashes/for when the music flows/ fire turns
to rainbows/prismatic screens of spectrum glass/riding
the high hat in some intertextual quiltwork of calligraphy
pens/scribing their maliferous etchings onto the blue notations
of pure colour/servo-mechanistic forces of nano-visions giving

sight to the impotent lens of blind telescopes/micro theories of cultures in contention/macro-theories of verbose finger puppets/scarifications of deep tyre tracks rolling across the dusty roads of a new frontier/these outlines of my lips in red chilli pepper/hot woman sauce/minkisi music/how I like my jazz!!!!/ribbons of peace doves taking to the air in an ontogonous migration of neo-surrealisms/optophones of some radical improvisation/reaching light years into the circle of things/the motion of motion in the motion of songs/kickin' it in the sound waves of your paradise/enter you pulchritudinous spirits into these smoke filled rooms of beatniks and peace pipes.

Dear Poet

Why you write that neo-surrealist
Intertextual quiltwork of untreated fabulation stuff
That seems to make no sense to man or beast
And gives me a headache trying to figure out
Why brothaz like you
Mr Ronnie McGrath
Anthony Joseph and Sun Ra
Be complicating things
And filling our headz with nonsense about
The African Origins of UFO's
"Breaking out the sky like the indelible mark of a comet"
Like an ankh"
Like the "Negro of my features is as absent as the pharaohs
    nose"
The "Provocative lips of your colouring pencils drowning in a
    watercolour"
Come on, man!
What's that about?
Lets face it!
You brothaz be getting praised
Be getting paid for Nothin!
And now white people be laughing at us
Thinking that we have truly lost our mindz in an
Outpouring of a perpetual search for the new
Thinking our body of literature is penned by four year olds in
    kente-cloths with dashiki patterns
Thinking our music isn't really music at all
Just a sound texture in search of form
YEAH!
Thanks to you
Ronnie McGrath

Thanks to you
Anthony Joseph
Thanks to you
Mr Kamau Braithwaite
Nathaniel Mackey
Bob Kaufman
Amiri Baraka
Clarence Major
Darius James
Ted Joans
Ornette Coleman
Cecil Taylor
Sun Ra
George Clinton
And the most out-there of you all (if there is such a thing in
    your feral bunch of Gypsies)
Mr Lee Scratch Perry and his "arkworks of inventions."
"I'm a toaster, not a boaster" indeed
Come on, Scratch,
What the hell are you playin' at?
It's 2010, MAN!!!!!!!!!!!
Can you all make some fuckin' sense—*PLEASE*!

Dear Reader

PEEPle be sZtukk
In their wayz
2 mch telvizion
& a lack of imaginashion
Stopping them frm dreeeeemin
A mch Bettah wirld than
they con-sum-e in alcho-pops
And mair-I-warna cunvirszations of
How high they wir the weak/week b4
& how they cdn't stop larfing frm the effekt of weeeed smowke

Stomach bus-sted open
twisted up
buckle-drunk on
krazzy ssshit powems
with ttwisted eyeballs tht cud'nt C strait

Their abstrakt thowt patterns
maykin them think
diffrently abowt themselvez
C-ing the worl 4 what it reel-y is
not perm-an-ent
or outside of clothes and L=A=N=G=U=A=G=E

Bt drezzed up in texts
in the illuzion of what they call sense & lojjikc
in the illuszzion of what they call formula
the countrees of their mindz in need of chaos and serendipity
need 2 loosen their limbz & pass the peace-pipe is whaat thay
    shld do

Dear ReAdER
B-leeve me when i say people
be stuk in their own shooze
their own clothes
wearin' 1 pair of glasses
& drinkin' frm their favourite cup
drivin their own karrs
to their OWN homes
to C THEIR CHILDREN
Bt stukkk in the lonely traffikk
By themselvz
Their musikk
An ipodic world of graate distance
Pluggin' them into even more lonliness
Their roadz leadin to nowhere
'cept from whenz they kame to go bck again
Mayke sense?????????????????????????

Her ankhles on a slipperless shoe / version I–one
A group sex experimentation

The radical poets are without work or home / reality has
won / tricked the living and poured their youth into pension
schemes / the women have covered their beauty with
makeup / piles and piles of even more illusion / the beauty
of their looks becoming myth / thinking they can hide
their tears in handkerchiefs / thinking they can straighten
their curves with bendy spoons / with hot metal spoons
heated on the backs of turtle shells / androgyny their will to
freedom and equality / the sexual revolution reduced to a
pill / reduced to a poet / her weapons / her words / without stone
to sharpen / defunct and workless / she spins like table tops
in search of clothes / in search of something more than his
gaze / his amputated fingers all over her body parts / all over
her poems / he is in her hair / entering her freckles with the
oversized shoes of an erect footprint / his presence / a thousand
mouse droppings of some countries invasion / armies of
himself looking for a fix / looking for a fit / she who is freaky
can have the glass slipper / be home around midnight / with
tales of one / two / three in a bed of crinkled sheets / of pillow
cases burning lawn crosses / strange fruit smells stinking
of smoked afro-wigs / picnic baskets in black man
pickle / marinated negro features / melanin paste mixed into
war paintings / like cave symbols sewn onto stone / pressed into
bone / the skin colourful tones of her poems radicalized / her
switchblade-lashes cutting glances out of sugar paper / carving
silhouettes into ether / outside the black-footed rain is
wounded / falls upon concrete and bleeds water stains / the salted
tears of impersonated sorrow songs / the swans flight is a noir
sheeted flow of spontaneous speech acts / iambic combustions
of gay morphemes in an haute couture of stanza patterns / a

marvellous display of showing off/in words of lace and frock
closets/her dog-collar truths untold/confession over/

Her ankhles on a slipperless shu / version II–2
4 Knee-O-su-ree-a-list powetz and Post-mow-dern academiks

Tha radikal powets R r without werk orh home/reel-al-i-ty haz
w1 /chrickt tha liv-ing & poured theyre yuuth in 2 pen=shion
skeemes/tha wu-men haave koverd thayre byooty with
mayke-up^/piles and piles of eevan more illuuzion/tha byooty
ov thayre looks B-cum-in mith/thin-king thay Kan hyde thayre
tayrzes in hnd-ker-cheefs/thin-king thay Kan strayten thayre
curves with bendi spoons/with hot metal spooonz heeted on
tha baks of tertle shells/an-dro-jiny thayre will 2 free√dum
and eqwaLitee/tha se-X-shoo-al revalooztion ree-doosed 2A
pill/ree-doosed 2A powit /heyr wepuns/heyr werdz/with-Δ-
owt stowne 2 shaarpen/deefunkct & werkless/s/he spinz lyke
tayble to♥ps in sertch of clozes/in sertch of sum-thing more
thahn hiz gayze/hiz am-pyoo-tated fin-gerz all o✲ver her bod-e
parts/all ov✲er her powimz/hee iz in→ her hair/Ntering her
freklz with tha O-vr-sized shooze of an Ereckt fut-pri-nt/his
prey♥zense/a thowzand mowse jjroppings of some count●ries
in-vayzion/Rmeez of him-cself looking for A fix/looking for
a fit/sheee whoo is freeeecky Kan have tha gl-ass slipper/ B
howme around◙ mid-nite/with taylze of 1one/ 2two/ 3three
in a bed of crin-kirled sheetz/of pill-O Kases burning lawn
††††crosses/stray-nje froot smellz stinking of smowked afro-
wigs/piknik bar-sketz in blk m●●●●●an pickle/marinated
ne●☺●gro feet-churz/melanin pay-ste mixed into war payn-
tingz/like cay-ve simblz sown onto stowne/pressed into
bowne/the skin cu-ler-ful tones of her powims radiKalized/her
switchblade-lashes cutting glances out of shoogar payper/car-v-
ing sil-how-ettes into eeeether/owt-c-ide thah bl●●●●●ak-footed
rayne is wooondid/fawlls ↑↑↑↑↑up↑on concreet and bleedz
water staynz/thah sawl-ted teerz of imper-sow-nait-ed so-rroe
songz/the swanz fly-t is a noir sheeted floe of spon-tay-nee-us
speech aKts/i-am-bik com-bus-tee-onz of g-ay morpheemz in

an awt coo-chture of stanza patt-ernz / a mar-v-lus diz-playe of
showin off / in werdz of layse and frok clozets / her dog-Kollar
trooths un-towld / con-fe-tion O-ver /

Her ankhles on a slipperless shoe/ version III–3
a found art poem

The radical poets are without work and home/it seems reality
has finally conquered the surreal/duped the artists and
tricked their elders into giving up their youth to the smoke
and mirrors of a sorcerer's pension scheme/construction is
a must/the myth of beauty piles makeup upon even more
makeup/creating an even bigger and better illusion/ Homage to
the billboards of advertising/outer worlds of curvaceous cyber
women shaped like spoons/hot spoons with an addiction to
veins/sex addicts doing it in their paradigms of neo-realisms/a
porncore illusion with stomachs like pregnant shells/with
stomachs like pregnant wombs/their shoes stuffed full of the
old woman's children/she who is a nursery rhyme/she who is
a tale/she who is an idea/a figment of my imagination/a sign
referring to itself/a reality in the guise of language/seeping
into conversation/into life narratives/under stones and into
poems/this page a verse cemetery/this book a tomb/I am the
pharaoh with an invisible nose/I am the pharaoh with an
African nose/I am the nose pharaoh/I am the pharaoh with
hot fleshy lips/my sex undefined/I speak in pyramids/in
a spoken soul/spitting geometry into microphones/my
footfall a song/twelve bar blues of unadulterated phunke/I
am the beginning/the middle/and the end of impalpable
things/a liquid modernity of strange juxtapositions/streams
of unfettered consciousness/cerebral/marvellous/fantastic
poems seeping out of the dark and dank mercurial waters
of electric daylight bulbs/subterraneous currents of pure
thought/wisdom of the wise and radical poets/without
work/without home/their genius hidden in some shallow
reality/selected poems of a conventional norm/keeping it
real/in the straight and narrowness of things/

[33]

Poem That Gets Up Nose & Into Arse-Crack Phunke

Black Poststructuralism 4 Bank Managers
and London Cab Drivers

how i dig writin'
crazee powim stuff
tht getz unda skin
and fin-ger-nayle
 up nowse and into arse-crak phunke

burr-o-win' deep
in-2 ware cayvez live
throo doorz
in-2 warrenz
in-2 house
lost in theez labi-rin-thyne twists and terns

deep
deep
deep-I-go

in-2 her sex juices/
in-2 her sex drivin' moanz lik/e Wynton's trum-pet-Ed
    black star -liner t2onze of
jah rastafari blazin fire pon-de bald headz

bt deeper stilL
in-2 the bus-ted vaynz of a john coltrane solow
wayre the dark deep owsh-anz
R black
& strong (currents)

miss-tee-ree-US
mer-Q-ree-AL &
straynge

cree-chures of sum ra-dee-kal ar(k)t work

ima-gi-nazion
so strong
ni-ther he-van
nor hell can ree-zide there

ima-gi-nazion
so strong
real-I-jhon kan't cum-peet.

Apertures Of The Soul In Sneak Preview
Ode to Jimi Hendrix

Cymbals of the high-hat hiss/spitting rhythm/spitting
cooking oil/into the hollow spines of passive zebras/chords
into gear/fired earth of a paradigm shift/nimble bass fingers
twisting engine keys/ outside this box are the radical plots
of a strange narrative/ idiosyncraticisms snaking sideways
in a subversive undertone/screams of inventions burst at the
seam as Jimi's guitar explodes into the cornucopiatic world
of beards and chicken feathers/ his conversations wrapped
in a blue note/singing in clusters of jazz music/singing in
clusters of the blues/singing in clusters of himself/dear
Jimi/the beautiful songs of your paintings make love to my
mouth like the recipe of food/textures of herbs and Caribbean
spices stand before me in a faint outline of the shadow boxers
dance routine/they say writin' is fightin'/so I am pulling out
my hair/just to stand with the sun flowers/so I can beam for
a while/ to smile/like a nanosecond in the light years of
thinking/as long as you do what you do/Jimi/there is hope/so
when I go out I want to sound like guy forks night/I want to
paint the sky with the ruby red lips of all my lovers/and with
God on my side/Allah/Buddah/Vishnu/Osiris/ omnipotent
systems of our necessary truths/omnivorous vehicles of our
faith/apertures of the soul in sneak preview/ sink me deep into
the rivers of some woman's thigh bone/the deep of her love
making/where dietys live and where the Mediators converse
in their tombs of tranquillity/their offerings/ libations to the
grand design of everything/Dear Jimi/I dance to your rhythm
with the splendour of song/authorial voice of your genius is a
Black church music yet to be born/shapes into circles/scalenes
of impregnable skin folds/equilateral moments of dense
solitude/octagons of desire/I'm digging your rendition of the
star spangled banner/love your geometry/ecludian gaze of

your greatest insight/new perspectives in search of the perfect angle/broken guitars of fretted necks/ music in flames of purple fire/guy forks night/'scuse me while I kiss the sky/

blk
brother
blk
british brother
afrodood
& afrodred
Love yr woo-man prowdly
& b kind 2 yr chill-jren
eet yr peeples foowde & live a lon-g blk life
Tayste all thin-gs blk with your cool blk mouth
reed a blk powim b 4 u go 2 bed
& reed a blk powim wen u wayke up in the morn-ing.

The DNA of an Other's Wig

Eyes bent back broken
Scraping against skin
Rich dark and golden
Follicles of hair
Laid to rest in the chemistry of warfare

Untangling these knotty radicalisms with pitch-fork and steel-
    tooth comb
Too black too strong aesthetic
Bleached out
Pushed into the languid silence of ether

Africa's backbone bent bleeding relaxed and limp with afro-
    sheen oil and disco gel
Imprinted on pillowcase
Blackening shirt collar rim
Mona Lisa's eye shadow smeared on Dyke & Dryden products

The centre of things
Mainstream and consumed by isms of
Black beauty on credit card
Extensions of my sister's hair borrowed
Her eyes
Lips
Teeth
And soul
On loan

Outsourced (Asia's got my Mojo/my nose bone/ankh-metal
    spine/my black stuff/APPROPRIATED)
Put it in the DNA of some 'other's' wig

Philipino slick with a Chinese shine
Misceginated melanin
Free of kink and twists
Of jungle talk
No room for foliage or bush hemp religion
Excavate your blue note/your flatten fifth
The spirited charge of your carnival and pan
MUTED.

Barber-shop man

You bitter cold sonofabitch Islander with the brutal hand of oppression
Trawling scalp
Trawling rainforests with your fine-tooth comb of knife wounds and razor blades
Bloody and sweet/
You a vicious island man / without wife and children / descendant of the overseer /
Smelling of bush meat and forest fires / plumes of infuriated smoke /
My head you have scraped into more poems / vitriolic poems and diatribes revisited /
I try to write with love for you / you my dashiki clad blue black brother smelling of revolution / perspiring the oil rich minerals of Africa's earth / I try to write in linear tongues of creole and class / in the high and low cultures of religion / nailed on the cross for you / we / we come with our pennies / we / we come with our childhood innocent and clean / we / we come with the shaky hands of our long fingers / we / we stood before you / bare-footed and quotidian folk / our music / a simple percussive drop of rain on the sun baked earth / we caribbean kings and queens in a plethora of carnival sequins / masters of our magic / high priests and priestesses of candomble / oguns children / shango's wrath imprinted on the soles of our dusty feet / we enter your shop / the Barber's shop / the hairy doorway of your hairy shop / your abattoir stepping over scalp / stepping over tripe / stepping over offal / over sous / over cow foot / fish head and tongue / the remnants of Massa's dinner table / enter your shop hungry but cheerful / marvel at the simple things / at ants crawling into crevice / at paint peeling off the wall in textures of black skin tones / in textures of shadism / in textures of

house and field negroes /marvel at old man Freddie talking to himself in whispers of some ancient Amharic language / at the muted violence of your razor blade cocked up in the sink like the lewd pose of a woman selling herself / marvel at the banal simplicity of razor sticky with soap / at the timid presence of Aston's mistress/ their affair an open secret /

Barber-shop man

You bitter cold sonofabitch
Islander with the brutal hand of oppression
Trawling scalp
Trawling rainforests with your fine-tooth comb of knife wounds and razor blades
Bloody and sweet/ ocean wrecker you / whale killer / expansionist /colonizer / polluter of planets / the violence of you in everything / you strong as an ox / your grip is a vice / cold metal fingers trawling scalp with comb not made for my kinky hair / with comb baptised in the cruelty of your disdain for island children / black Diasfrican's scattered like seeds unwanted across a barren land / cruel barber shop man your soul the dark insensitive night of malice / pain you have encomiumised / your cruel god fights with my god / and she / no match for my mothers strength / no match for mama's toil / the pain of lives endured / the men of her broken heart strings penning sorrowful songs to the barren gates of vacuous yards / / she my mother Africa barefooted and regal in her stride / wide hipped and full breasted woman come for me quick / this man is evil /this man is evil / pitching Delilah against Sampson / broken flower stems uprooted / my hair gone /eyez tearful /come grandmother / come for me quick / come for me

[42]

quick / I am weak / I am weak and awaiting your protection/I am weak and awaiting your kiss.

Untitled

I look into the process of your making
and see illusions that i'm attracted to

beauty isn't always natural
but all the same
beauty is sure enough beautiful—*when she is a woman*

the eye of the beholder
your eyez
the eye of the beholder
my eyez
our eyez beholding beauty

marvellous conceptual abstract thing
pulled across my face
flesh and bone art of religion
genteel art high on culture
black aesthetic art bold as radicalism
nose and lip art of representation
conceptual artwork in a Black beauty shop language of
    history and erudition

the peoples art of makeup and marketing
their jewellery and clothes
hair pressed to a shine
devoid of herstory
devoid of kink
BLING!

Creationation I

dance
petal feet you glorious fish scale
limb sturdy as shell bone
white water optics
the rippled effect of movement and sand dunes
of transference and motion
restless foot magic
irresistible
flux

Jig

Growing up on music
We grew wings on our feet and flew
Made a pact with movement and discovered geometry

Shaped our bodies out of triangles
Equilateral timbres of the choreographer's song colonized our
Hearts and we were hooked on her rhythm

She showered us in paradise
Took our hard earned laughter to a place where happiness
    resides
So we gave her gold
And we gave her diamonds
And the ancestors looked up with joy in their eyes
Pleased with what we had become
Pleased with our toil
Pleased with our invention
Pleased with our motivation to-keep-on-keeping-on in the face
    of adversity
What faith you have / they said / speaking from a crystal ball

She threw a set of bones on the floor and I watched in
    amazement
As the magic revealed itself to our feet

Claiming our bodies from the labour of capitalism
We danced Rumba and we danced Guaguanco
Krumpin' our sculptured black limbs until they body-popped
    and Lindy-hopped to the phunke that had taken control of
    our minds

Hypnotized the Gods one night with a Juba routine
Stepped to the plate and resurrected the Nicholas brothers
Gregory Hines was there
Mr Bo Jangles saw him moon walking on water
Said he was no ordinary dancer
More like a magician
Yes I said
He is one of those Griot people who comes from the future
I saw him on the high street tagging walls with his tap shoes
Clapping with the soles of his feet
Writing poetry with the tip of his grandfathers tongue

And moving towards me our souls collide
Gregory and me choreographied
Alvin Ayleyfied
Garth Faganized
& for that one night on an Essex dance floor
In a club called *The Lacy Lady*
I / like my fellow brothers and sisters
Was omnipotent

Philosophy, Religion, Race, Death, Our Father, In Laws, School, Big Brother, Mother, Ex-Girlfriend, Poetry, Black Publisher, The Black Playwright, bredrin

PHILOSOPHY

All I want to do
Is bring some good in the world
But people
Are afraid of my poems
Knowing that I will say it
And keep on saying it
Because that's the truth

RELIGION

Worship her feet
Body and soul
My wife
Daisy

RACE

Proud of my hair
My lips
My nose
My beautiful skin
But this 'blackness'
This 'blak' thing
Is a burden.

DEATH

My brother was a god/good man
Kind
Extremely brave
Went out on his own—*wasn't there when he needed me*
That day I failed
GREATLY.

OUR FATHER

Drink gets the best of him
Speaks too loud when drunk
And cries at the fact that
He doesn't know how to
Hold his granddaughter
This educated man
Reads a rightwing newspaper
And doesn't trust books.

IN LAWS

If only they knew
The troubles I've seen.

SCHOOL

Got punched in
My chest by the deputy head teacher
Crashed into his desk and fell to the ground
My head bleeding
Got up and cursed him
His mother
His sister
His entire nation
Years would pass before I discovered
Richard Wright
And James Baldwin.

BIG BROTHER

Look up to him
Checked ourselves out and embraced black consciousness
Sometimes it's really hard to keep on keepin' on in this world
But we are Malcolm's children
Garvey's got our backs
Martin has shown us how to love.

MOTHER

I wish she knew my father
Could tell me where I'm from
How I'll go bald
Will she never speak to her sister again?
Some say he was married.

EX-GIRLFRIEND

We were a perfect match
Working class
Oppressed and subjugated
Got educated together and fought society
Discovered race politics
Discovered feminism
Then she went her way
And I went mine.

POETRY

Okay! Okay!
So you can only afford to pay
the musician
Well how about the poet, man
He'll need some water
it's hot as hell in here.

BLACK PUBLISHER

Look, brother
You're an excellent poet
And we can just about get away with that abstract stuff
But the race and feminism back to Africa material
That I'm not so sure about
Too angry
Too angry, man
Can't you just write some shit about love and shit?

THE BLACK PLAYWRIGHT
Poem for Kwame Kwei Armah

My GRIOT brother you are perfect
True to the bone and perfect
The epitome of Black perfection
Facing your adversity with an elegance reserved for jazz
You are more perfect than a poem
You are more perfect than the complete works of Shakespeare
My female God envies your perfection
Perfect brother with an African name
Your transition is perfect
But be careful as you go in this imperfect world of imperfect
    people
For they know that you are perfect
That you are sheer perfection
And nothing more.

BREDRIN

Dear artist friend of mine
Where are you now?
Not painting like you should be
But fucked up and bitter *(the glass ceiling is a whore)*
Knowing that your unexamined sense of self
Imprisons your ability
To understand
The rhythm of your dreams.

Her Patois is Montage

The girl who tastes like eye candy siphons blood vessels for a
living/kidnapping tongues is her favourite pastime/the killer
of conversation/she who sterilises gossip with her shoes/she
walks the talk of television/speaking in a broken English/her
patois is montage/she thinks in a way her pictures want to
speak/misrepresentations follow her home/colonise her
narrative/raise her children in a culture of screens/the mirrors
of themselves imitating art in the heaven and the hell of some
gangsters paradise/exiled here with this lonely crowd/her
soul in need of company/religion is not enough/is never
enough for all the pain/the sky is an empty sphere/devoid of
Brahma/Vishnu/Olokun/Ogun/devoid of theology/the dead
spirits of Beelzebub have risen again/she no longer believes in
cloud machines/rain dance/or mumbo jumbo subtitles/taking
her head to a different height/outside of poetry/surfing
on rainbows with her eyelashes/her pot of gold is a visa
card/the hole in the wall of her purse strings are controlled by
Washington/Condoleezza lives large/Condoleezza lives an
opulent lifestyle/ Condoleezza eats rice with her fingers/
Condoleezza eats rice with the fingers of her beautifully
painted nails/Condoleezza is a cultured woman/she has a lot
of ethnic-quette/Condoleezza hates my poems/thinks they
are a cipher/some sort of a coded revolution in verse/a black
revolutionary verse speaking in Malcolm rhythm/Condoleezza has
a lot of friends in high places/I can no longer read my poems in
public/Condoleezza has put a block on me/everybody is scared of
what I might say/I will have to tone it down/fight and run away/
so I can live to fight another day/fight and run away/so I can live to
fight another day/fight and run away/so I can live to fight another
day/the girl who tastes like eye candy siphons blood vessels for
a living/kidnapping tongues is her favourite pastime/the killer

of conversation/ she who sterilises gossip with her shoes/she walks the talk of television/speaking in a broken English/her patois is montage/she is pure poetry/

I slip into the solitude of a blank page

Where meaning is lost to the grand postmodernisms of an
    immaculate
Implosion
The birth of my Christ is a riotous noise
Her thunder
The nakedness of rocks falling
The collapse of everything
Man woman and child torn from their reference sites

The outstretched hand of a bleak future my only way home
Reality surrounds me and yet
I am made in the image of some woman's clothes
The beauty myth of our racial fears constructed
Like the artifice of dread-locks twisted onto the
Consciousness of black and white freedom fighters

Twisted into the outer-national imaginings of new diasporas
Joining hands in a circuitry of esoteric drum patterns
The skin and bone of rhythm makers working their magik
Speaking in tongues
Tongues with spears sticking out of them
African tongues of ancient EGYPT
Black pharaoh tongues
Drum and bbbbbbass tongues possessing your souls
Bending your earlids wide open
Pouring sheet metal musik into it
Pouring sheet metal musik into it

Contemporary Britain
The sparkling wine of Philosophunk
Bouncing off the sunlight in an ecstasy of rave tablets

Looking for Woodstock in the aftershock of nuclear head
  explosions
Sounding out of Jimi's guitar like polyphonic ringworms
  burrowing into the dense mediascape of sound creatures
  morphing into a Jackson Pollock take on things

Jimi and Pollock
Hendrix and jack framing their agony in the blue genius of
  space probes
Looking for the new
For the Ra
For the Chi
For the Yin and the Yang
Equilibrium complete

Brass Fantasy

Deep into the future of the here and now/history has aged
before my eyes of natural laws and witnesses/grown old
and fragile/shaky truths unfixed by the irascible charge of
revolution/stripped to the bone of dead narratives/naked as a
myth in this negroblack constructed world of my ephemeral
selves/I think therefore I think I am/FREE!/invisible chains
of my captivity is a culture of hidden text messages/the
omnipresence of a complicit silence to throw overboard/the
dissenting voice of poetry/its black is beautiful discourse
of Rastafarianism/burns fire on the maleficent spirits of
pregnant slave ships/burns fire on the bloated stomachs of
dormant food mountains/burns fire on the excessive habits
of free trade/burns fire on . . . /burn baby burn with your
seraphic tongues of nyabingi church music/burn baby burn
your flames of decolonisation/exorcising the mind with
knowledge of santeria/vodun/Olodumare/cascading out of a
cowrie-shell marketplace in the signs and the symbols of ebony
medicine men/Rah-doms of black pharaohs in their pyramids
shaped like time machines/reaching for the stars/deep
into the future of the here and now/masters of their own
invention/masters of space travel/their Nubian technologies
are the grand designs of preservation/are the grand designs
of self preservation/we live in centuries at a time/and we
speak in the past and the present of our music/overtures in a
cacophony of gospel singers/speaking in biblical tongues of
spirit possession /Shango's thunder is the lone tower blocks
of our grime/the eighteenth floor of our class struggle/the
chalked outlines of dead suicide notes pushing babies out of
bullet holes/into these hierarchies of intense suffering/legacies
of broken families amputated by the middle passage of hooded
time bandits/the blind future of an aged youth culture drunk

on media theory/high on gynesis/sexed up by the sexualisation
of violence/monstrous feminines in their virtual worlds of
crack-crystal-capitalism/mining sugar cubes/oh the sweet life
of the dead living/looking for gold in the illuson of brass/

Perpendicularities in Fetishes of Rubber and Brass

Burnt embers of steam tainted with its own guilt/upward and rising like a flame in the phoenix of conscious women/silhouettes in the holes of impossible songs/the pain of your beauty is an opaque melancholy/a rude outline of some womanist fiction inscribed upon the lips of indomitable fountain pens/your flesh/a textwork quilt in polysemic skin tones of a Spanish guitar/protruding from the hips like a curvaceous outer flow of gendered body parts/scalpel blades of a dark invention/conjuring cyber whores/the provocative yoga positions of their collective spirit is a sexed up maths formula/perpendicularities in fetishes of rubber and brass/their fingers smelling of religion/the liquid orgasm of an enriched tongue food sliding in the up-stream of men/where water appears in the guise of rain fall/neo-expressionisms of spheric glass capsules/the textured clouds of their invention tasting like candyfloss/brush strokes of a complex illusion/the conjurer's magic in free fall/the conjurer's magic in free verse/the conjurer's magic set free/the end of narrative/and all that is broken can be moulded into new abstractions/made proper and fixed again/like the sticks and stones of a woman's heart beat/the broken embers of a life in drag/and what a drag this life of skin clothes/prosperity and makeup/neurotic lip pencils shaped like a penis/her mouth a cave in the fascism of his sex drive/war and beauty collide as le mouvement feminine explodes like a Barbie doll's implant/everywhere tits and arse speaking in an ad campaign/everywhere plastic/fake hair of man-made fibres trembling like a vibrator in the osculums of the pornographers lens/profiles of a rare snake bite/species of wrath/her venom/the spitefulness of barbed wire twisted into the curse of her servitude/

Spiral Beauty Out of Control

I am not the Afrocentric night/weighted as a curtain/dark as a dream/exploding into nightmares/blood filled moments of terror and klans-women with picnic baskets on their heads/blue black essentialism set in stone and ardent whites of power and hierarchy/anger and bitterness unfolding into the cotton sheets of institutional racism/the textured silence of dense hypocrisies negotiating greed/mountainous debts in plumes of fascist flower arrangements/stenched upon denizens in cloak filled pockets of immaculate emptiness refusing mouths and shanty town writings/imaginary sex workers and their imaginary clients in dialogues of lewd exchanges/blue pornographies silhouetted against phallic outlines of erect church steeples/heaven bound and pyramid conscious songs/

I am not celebrity stricken or driven by the ego of camera flash and sex messages/neither cheap or expensive things entertain my wants or can seduce my desires/nepotisms prejudice grant no favours to the sturdy moons of my nihilism and anarchy/bribes in abstractions of deep and ravenous pockets are detested here/by me/ and the many men who are beyond the fantastic dreams of false promises/thrown out of the principled/luminous/sun burnt feathery shades of the choice to be me/and the many/and the infinite/numerous you/atomistic peoples in shells of unfilled solitude/screens/and text messages/always/more text messages/ciphers of some green and wiry thought/contemplating dollar signs/

I am not against women/their body parts/or their looks/the spiral beauty of their soul steeped in a baptism/wet water of thought and profundity/complex attractions in gowns of sexuality/same sex workers of a same sex world/thinking

their same sex thoughts / like the same sex people thinking
their sexed up other thoughts / and women / always women
and Freudian dreams / always women and sex / and sex and
women / and sometimes men who like other men / and
sometimes men who murder men for loving men / and men
and sex are the cries of war / tentacles of some death trap
machine / and the rape of villages / and the broken wings
of fragile children / and fascism is a man / and murder is a
man / and nightmare is a male dream narrated by a man / and
the poet is a man / omniscient poet sewing words into his
language / communication is a conduit to other men / and god is
a man / is a man / is a mans religion /

The Rainbow of Her Beauty

In the celebrity of
Camera-shoots
And magazine covers

Bare breasted models
Inflate their lips with
The frantic cries of billboard messages

Thin but not quite waif enough
To dine with butterflies
The faceless strings of their hidden beauty
Sharpen scalpel-blades

As the plastic surgeon
Sturdy as a hungry penis makes an incision
And pours the wealth of stockbrokers
Into their teenage thighs

And as the secrets of their thongs
Peek out of hipster-trousers
Titillating monsters

The schoolyards of their innocent years
Throw dead skipping ropes
Into the tears of polluted riverbeds.

The Theory Of Everything

Abstract veins of colourful guitar strings entwined
Around the fingerless patterns of a joyful noise
Where flowers grow and spirits make their way to the
    paradise
Of a songbirds vocal chords pouring sheet liquid music into
    the
Raw experimentation of day breaking across the cityscape
Like a blunt torchlight looking for you in the lonely crowd of
Gentrification rolling across the urban diasporas like millions
    of black folk thrown to the breeze of a perfect song
    fashioned into the armour of performance poets seducing
    microphones with their ego's stuffed in the arse of some
    guys promise to publish movie houses and MTV dreams
    hijacking the visual landscape with even more talk of
    keeping it real and getting paid in the fullness of beer
    barrels screaming
COME ON ENGLAND!
COME ON ENGLAND!
COME ON ENGLAND!
Into this brave new world of racial tolerance
Where black on black violence is the order of the day and no
    one gives a fuck about the colour of her lipstick
For it's the quality of her blowjobs and the anal sexualisation
    of many women that will see us through this laddish
    moment of four wheel drives and soaring house prices
    mouthing it off
Like some bourgeois education package
Selling dead novels to the educated fools of Sunday morning
    breakfast readers
Adding more newspapers to the sugar of their cornflakes
With the spoons of their silver mouths

Drunk on the belief that they were born to swim in egg yoke
and dip their coffees in a toast to the shadowy world of
long champagne glasses
Turning gold to liquid
Liquid to cash
Cash to assets
Assets to the war of a terrible orgasm throwing
Knives into the violence of some woman's mouth.

A Poem For Literary Critics Who Like Their Whisky Neat

Memories of me did not know books until late /and poetry
was far from me then/the world hidden in some other
place/outside of school/outside of my school/outside
of head/outside of my head/outside of books for second
class citizens/my university/the party where Africa was
murdered/and where girls painted sores on the lips of their
vagina houses/invited men into their mouths/invited men
into their homes/many men with many mouths/hungry
for poetry recitals/she who is barely a woman/heavy with
stanza and iambic pentameters/the blue glass rain of her
conversations speaking in free-sex driving lessons/sullied
now/but had she not eaten the seeds of dried apple cores/she
would have been virgin for at least a day/the red flames of
these holy candles cannot cleanse her reputation/miss
representation is a voyeur/she will follow her home/follow
her to the redundant springs of a nineteen sixties water
bed/nail her to the cross of some holy communion/her
lipstick badges smeared with decadent kisses that belong
to some sticky-fingered earth worm practice/ memories of
me did not know books until late /and poetry was far from
me then/the world hidden in some other place/outside of
school/outside of my school/outside of head/outside of
my head/outside of books for second class citizens/and the
educated have their road maps/they can read the bones/the
signs are good to them/the stars shine out of their ~~arseholes~~
ear-holes/planets constellate around their pocket books/they
pick their nails at the table of progress/wipe their tiny
mouths on the rims of rusty circles/ they have witchdoctor
cloaks that can turn ideas into a PhD language/academician
talk of freemasonry/their voodoo is a priest/his dog-collar
truths opening doors that lead to other doors/windows of a

blind opportunity/sucking on the eyeballs of my past/where memories of me did not know books until late/and poetry was afar.

Sez

Black poem
Black British poem
Reveal yourself whole

What do you look like
Feel like
Taste like

Are you lost in abstraction or ~~reel 2 reel~~ real as logic
Mimesis or a Diegesis poem

In or outside of genre/colour/class
What is your L=A=N=G=U=A=G=E / man
For whom do you speak / brother!

Postcolonial space poem
FIXED OR UNFIXED
In between of what
YEAH! That's what you are
(A) Political poem

Position paper poem
Position paper poetry
That's what they say you are

Who sez
Who se z what!
Where
When
Why
Who

Whoo
whooo
Sez z z z

Black NEO-surrealist DADA poetry you are—*NO*
Acoustic avant-gardista poem you are—*NO*
Black aesthetic poem you are—*NO*
Langston blues poem you are—*NO*
Black nationalist poem you are—*NO*
Postmodernist contagious poem you are—*NO*
Jazz poem
Beat poem
Drum and bbb-bass poem
Non-specific Grime poem

Elusive poetry
Outside the frame
Outside of narrative
Prolepsis poetry
Contemporaneous poetry
Beyond the canon poetry
MARGIN-alized poetry

I know

I bet you're a love poem!
I bet you're a female poem pressed against my lips

I can

I can smell your perfume
Your womanist fiction is written all over this verse

I bet you're a gay poem
A Good As You poem
A black lesbian poem
Your feminisms ahead of its own time
What was it that Audre said
Seboulisa / the warrior poet

'it is better to speak, knowing that we were never meant to survive.'

Dark Countries In
Nude Outlines Of The Feminine Slipper

Woman stitched with emotion
Me and you joined
To muscle
To bone
To lips and love making
Fluids in up-stream trails of wet lipstick

Smeared

On linen
On clothes
Beneath fingernails
Between the joy and the pain of vibrant rainbows
Between the joy and the pain of climax and heat
Incubated silk worm tablets tasting of lace

The deep skin folds of your miss-tery
A seductive embroidery pattern in fingerprints of rainforests
Planted on your thigh
My presence on your presence

Your womanscape shaped like the land
Dark country in nude outlines of the feminine slipper
The funk tasting rain like flesh on my tongue
Woman flesh and a mouth full of language
Woman flesh and a mouth full of poetry
I talk
fuck
eat
& bleed
For

My
    Christ.

Canon Fire Is A Blind Institution

Reifications of blue sky people injected into the veins of my plasma screen/The taxonomy begins with stereotypes of the tragic mulatto morphing into the coonery of her mammies smile/One drop too dark for the ripples of her own signification/the post traumatic syndrome of her slavery resides in the gangsters paradise of a new media/of a new screen culture of disinformation/Where the 4x4s of their lyrics is a false consciousness/Trick bags of style over content steering me away from curiosity/Steering me away from these books/Into the matrix of a directors cut/i am groomed and remade in the silhouettes of a one dimensional man/Seduced by the shimmering effects of baking foil/Windows of escapism hidden in a rock crystal/The crack fiend of her broken womb is an abused childhood of under aged sex workers and radical pole dancing/Alcoholism the language of her curses/Knife fighting the colour of her rage/Barbed wire the texture of her lovemaking/She who is pimpnotized by the seductive lure of pixel screens/game boys and game girls in a vicious game of head hunting/Simulacrums of reality/Broken off/Amputated from the real of ether/i pause in the hope that i am far too crazy to go insane/i pause in the hope that the Godfather of this philosophunk will suddenly step forward and take me to the bridge/break it down like a Lindy Hopper popping off in a spasmodic moment of hip hop fantasm/so i can jump off/ into the baptism of dead suicide notes/poems from the flies of stench and greed/the chalked outlines of their insect bodies smelling of formaldehyde/is this really art or just another Damien Hirst take on things?/The selective genius of their canon fire is a blind institution/An art for art sake politics of occupation/My belly full of ideas and yet i am hungry for revolution/the messengers feet is warm against my lips/The freshness of our blood is the coded verse of an hermetic text/His is an ancient wisdom blown from the future/predictions of Malcolm/Martin/Medgar/murdered/Tragedy is the sorrow of a perditious angel/fallen/Broken into fragments of blue melancholy/ History is much more than the little folks of a grand narrative/Much more than Baraka/Kaufman/Joans/Breton/Much more than a poet/Much more than poems/Much more than the sum of itself/Beyond food stamps/Beyond the heights of food mountains/Beyond the text/outside of it all/Ostracised/ignored/

In The Neon Signs Of . . .

Style is the way
My chisel falls with grace
Upon the rock of a hard knock life
As I try to carve a poem out of stone

Chipping away at the brutal reality of grand hallucinations
At the fake laughter of bold text messages
Calling all poets to the open-mimicry of another election
   campaign
Lacking any real sense of choice and freedom

And their strings are as visible to me now as the scars that
   her
Face is carved from
As visible to me now as the once invisible prison of a glass
   ceiling
Much sturdier than a whites only sign
In a whites only world of cultural imperialism

Of blak teenagers styling themselves in the name of cultural
   mediators
And cool hunters
In search of user friendly blak folks
To deliver wiggermatographic movie houses
A corporate cool
And boys with bullets
Shooting from their mama's stomachs
Like the riotous noise of shock and awe printed on their
   T-shirts

In the neon signs of
AMANI
GUCCI
VERSACE
STATUS SYMBOLS

Hyper realer than reality itself posing as catwalk models
Walking the walk in the talk of tell-lie- vision
Where the beautiful people are as pretty as coke lines
Burying coffins in the cave of a young man's nose
As he comes up for air in the appropriated fusion of his
    clothes

His language
The symbolic twists of his hair
Styled and re-packaged in a super new formula
Of super cool baby milk

Genetically modified
For the false aspirations of breast implants sexualising the
    surgeons knife
In a grotesque re-styling of Negro features

Circles of Polysemy

Dear Poets & friends
I speak to you in verse
Because truth is subjective
Your decoding is another encoding
& so it seems
                    We go around
In circles of polysemy
Each to their own patois
Sucking on our own tongues
Trying to understand
The meaning of life
Trying to grab a hold
Of what isn't really there

We are neither fixed
Or unfixed
        By love
        Chains
        Or racial codes

        But out there
In the in-between of things

        Where the lies unfold
            And poetry hurts.